D1146685

About the Author
Professor Georgie Blink

Professor Georgie Blink (BSc, MSc, PhD, Dip. Drag, OBE), studied at London University, Harvard, and the Centre for Advanced Dragon Studies in Vladivostock. She is a world expert on dragons, and a founding member of the International College of Serpentology. She now lives near Bristol, England, with an 85 year old Stumptailed Bolonka dragon called Picton. The professor has kept dragons since childhood and is a regular contributor to many dragon owner helplines and newsletters. The Professor and Picton are available for occasional visits to well-fireproofed schools.

www.professorblink.co.uk

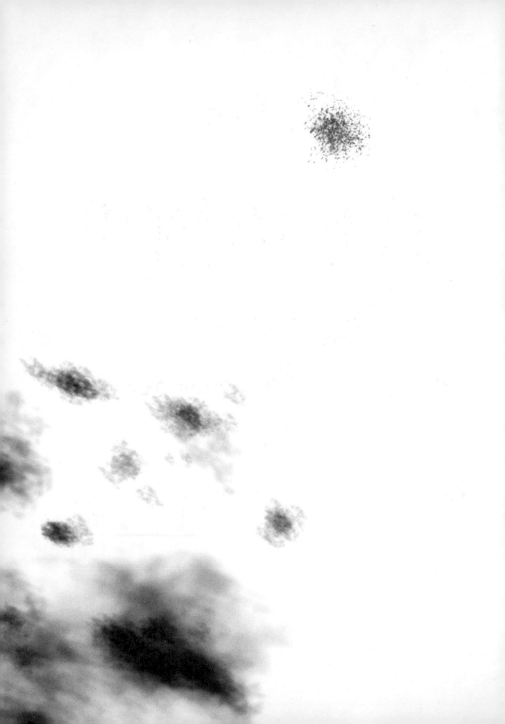

My First

Pet Dragon

The Complete
Handbook for
Beginners

In memory of Frances Broun-Lindsay

Special thanks to Sarah Weavers and
Rob and Kit Gore Langton

Amanda Mitchison

My First

Pet Dragon

The Complete
Handbook for
Beginners

Professor Georgie Blink

Edited by Amanda Mitchison

Illustrated by Andy Rowland

CATNIP BOOKS
Published by Catnip Publishing Ltd.
14 Greville Street
London EC1N 8SB

First published 2008
1 3 5 7 9 10 8 6 4 2

Text copyright © Amanda Mitchison, 2008
Illustrations copyright © Andy Rowland, 2008

The moral rights of the author and illustrator have been asserted

A CIP catalogue record for this book is available from the British Library

ISBN 978-1-84647-066-0

Printed in Poland

www.catnippublishing.co.uk

Contents

Chapter 1

Dragons as Pets

If you are reading this you and your family have most probably decided to keep a pet dragon. This is a brave decision. Dragons make challenging and unusual pets. They can provide hours of entertainment and make very good guard animals. You will never be burgled if you have a dragon.

However dragons are not easy pets. You will need to show courage and determination. But, if handled firmly and given clear boundaries, your dragon can become a very interesting pet. So persevere. The first years are the hardest and there is nothing like living a little dangerously. But at all times remember to follow the safety instructions carefully.

Before you bring a dragon into your life there are a few things you should think about:

Do you have the time to look after your dragon?

You will need to feed your dragon every morning and evening and give it daily flying and petting. The den will need to be cleaned out twice a week.

Can you afford a dragon?

Dragons are not cheap to keep. There are considerable set up costs – especially for larger breeds.

Remember your dragon will always want the best – their tastes in food and entertainment are expensive. It will also want fresh changes of jewellery and you must not skimp on fire extinguishers.

There will also be vet bills, pet insurance fees, and the costs of training and anger management courses.

Do not forget the hidden costs. Your parents will need to budget for repairs – even with the best disciplined dragons, there will be some degree of fire damage.

Dragon droppings can be sold at a premium, so it is worth investing in a dropping's jar for easy collection. This will go some way go some way to offsetting other costs.

Do you have many visitors?

Remember that dragons do not like strangers and can lash out. You will need to put up warning signs at the front door. If you live in a flat, you should get the consent of neighbours.

Bon Voyage

Going on holiday

Only very rarely will you be able to take your dragon with you when you go on holiday. Airlines and train companies will refuse to take dragons on board for safety reasons and most campsites and bed and breakfasts are not at all dragon friendly.

Are there local dragon kennels? Do you have brave relatives living nearby who are not house proud and would enjoy the chance to dragon sit?

There are all sorts of hazards to travelling with dragons. Every year I receive hundreds of letters from owners who get into trouble abroad. This letter should be a warning to us all...

Cairo Central Prison

Dear Professor Blink,

We couldn't find a kennel for simpkins, our Carpathian schlange dragon. so when we flew to south Africa last year, for a short winter break, I gave her a sleeping pill, wrapped her in aluminium foil and we snuck her through security and onto the aeroplane.

Everything was fine for the first couple of hours but then simpkin's sleeping pill must have worn off. suddenly sirens started to blare. The flight attendants ran up and down the aisle in a panic. It turned out that simpkins had crept out of the overhead luggage compartment and made her way to the toilets. Here she had, naturally, been breathing fire and had set off the alarms.

We did an emergency landing in Cairo where Geoffrey, Simpkins and I were arrested. We have been in prison here ever since. The food is horrible and we are getting very thin. Poor Simpkins has lost her spark.

Please don't be tempted to stowaway your dragon or you might end up like us.

Sad Regards, Penny Bunstead,

PS Simpkins asks if you could please send him some caviar.

Chapter 2
Things you will need

Bedding Treasure: jewellery, aluminium foil, marbles, gold drawing pins, sturdy Christmas decorations, silk and velvet.

Bicarbonate of Soda—in case of emergencies

Cleaning materials (paint scraper, dustpan and brush, scourer, bucket and cloth)

Collar and Extendable Lead.

The Den — Two well made ovens or metal
boxes lined with fibreglass insulation, or
for larger breeds a custom – made den.

Deodoriser — a must!

Droppings tray (preferably metal)
and droppings collection jar.

Extractor Fan

Facial shield

Fire blanket, fire bucket and water or foam fire-extinguisher: do not use carbon dioxide or wet chemical fire-extinguishers.

Food — dragon biscuits as the mainstay. But dragons enjoy any food as long as it is expensive: white and black truffles, olives, caviar, raspberries, lobsters, Parma ham, lychees and other tropical fruits, etcetera.

Food Dishes — heavy earthenware food dishes are best – they are fireproof and cannot get knocked over.

Grooming Aids — tweezers, cotton buds, scale polisher, buffing cloth, grooming brush, dishcloths, clippers.

Padlock and Chain

Oven Gloves

Travelling cage

Treats — fizzy water, smelly cheese.

Toys — pink princess dolls, plastic knights, spinning tops, a trombone.

Dragon Don'ts

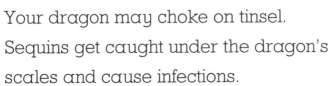

■ *Never* use sequins or tinsel.

Your dragon may choke on tinsel.
Sequins get caught under the dragon's
scales and cause infections.

■ *Never* clean with pine
scented disinfectant.

Your dragon will find the smell
disturbing and will not settle at night.

■ *Never* give your dragon rubber balls —
your dragon will choke on them as they
melt in its throat. Dragons do enjoy

catching – games so why not try a fireproof Frisbee? They are available from some high street toy stores.

Chapter 3
The Den

Dragon pet-shops sell insulated dens in a variety of sizes. But for the dwarf or medium-sized breeds, two disused ovens welded together will do just as well, at a fraction of the price. Otherwise two metal boxes, thoroughly insulated with fibreglass and aluminium foil, can make a cosy den.

Droppings

Droppings should be collected in a small tin tray. Do not use a plastic tray, as it will melt.

Where to keep the den

Your parents will probably not allow you to keep your dragon in the kitchen or dining room because of the smell. Ideally your den should be in a fireplace so that the smoke and fumes can rise up the chimney. But utility areas, or garages will do fine. Do not put your dragon's den into or near to a bathroom or toilet. Dragons are obsessed with human bodily functions and enjoy lighting natural

gases. You will not feel comfortable using the bathroom with a dragon scratching on the door.

Fire Precautions

It is essential to have a fire-extinguisher, fire bucket, fire blanket and first aid kit near to the den. Always place the den on top of bricks, fireproof ceramic tiles or concrete. Heat from an angry dragon can penetrate even the best insulated den and burn tables or linoleum.

Padlocks

Your padlock must be sturdy and tamper proof. Dragons are smart and can break any code, so whatever locking system you have must be based on keys or remote control.

DRAGON DON'TS

■ *Never* put your dragon, even temporarily, in a guinea pig or rabbit hutch.

■ *Never* let your dragon set up its own informal nest in the living room. Every night your dragon must be padlocked into its den.

PROFESSOR BLINK SAYS: A LOCKED-UP DRAGON IS A HAPPY DRAGON!

I get tired of telling readers that they must keep their dragons out of the bathroom. I had to write a very stern reply to this letter:

> The Messy Room with Spiderman Wallpaper,
>
> rkside Avenue, Togglepuddle.
>
> Dear Gorgy,
>
> I am riting to you from my bedroom. The door is locked. All my compooter games have been confiskated. And I am

not allowed to watch television for 1000 years.

This is why. Last week my orribel Oncle Arther came to visit. Oncle Arther is The Worst Relatif Ever Ever Ever. He has a huge red face and a monster size mostache which always has bits of carrot stuck in it. He calls me boyo and asks me diffikolt sums and laffs when I cannot do them.

So this time, just for a trik, I hid Fluffy our young dwarf blutgnasher, behind a towil in the toylet. At supper Orrible Oncle Arthur, as per usual, finished his chips and sawsidges and beens in a nanosecond and burped.

I said Dear oncle, would you care for some more beens?

He said well thank you boyo that is very kind of yoo to ask. And while we are on the subject of beens, let me ask a kwik question. If I had 12 tins of baked beens and eech been woz six millimetres long and I opend all 12 tins and put each been nose to tail with the been in front of it. How many beens would I need to encircle the earth?

I said I didn t know and gave him four spoonfuls of fart making beens, not one. When he had slurped up the beens, he made a deep rumbling noise and asked to be exzcused.

I pritendid to have sumthing to do and went and listnid in the hall. I could heer him rumbling away in the toilet. The methane gas was building up! Would Fluffy do the job and light up those farts?

Suddenly, all in a sekund, came a sound of roaring flames, and a screem AAAAAAAAAAAAAAAAAAAAAAAAAAAA AAAAAAAAGGGGGGGGGGGGGHHH!

Dad foursed the toylet door open. The walls were black with soot and the floor woz covered in broken glass and Fluffy lookt reelly sheepish. Out of the windoo that woz broken we saw oncle Arther running for his life, he woz clutching his backside and screeming. He jumpt the bacvk fence and sped off into the park

Dad said Poor Arther, look how fast he is running. Soon

he will go into orbit!

I tried not to smile. I said How long will it take him to encircle the earth?

My stressipants Mum glared at me. Go to yoor bedroom!

Fluffy is now in a dragon rescue centre. We will never see him again! If you meet him, say hello from me.

From Max

Chapter 4

Buying Dragons

If you have taken the plunge and decided to have a pet dragon you have three choices: you can buy an egg, or a ready hatched dragonlet. Alternatively you can adopt a rescue dragon. The choice you and your family make will depend, of course, on your circumstances and the time of year. But each choice has its advantages and its pitfalls.

Dealers and Paperwork

Whether you chose an egg, a dragonlet or a rescue dragon, always use a Dragon Club registered dealer. Ask to see the dragon's Breeding Card which will give you your dragon's pedigree. You don't need to buy a show dragon — many mixed breeds make excellent dragons. But it is essential to check the pedigree for man-eating tendencies. You should demand at least three generations of non man-eating dragons.

In the case of dragonlets and rescue dragons, you should also be given its Dragon Club Misdemeanours and Damages Report. This is particularly important in the case of a rescue dragon.

NEVER
NEVER BUY A DRAGON
THAT HAS NO PAPERWORK
NEVER BUY A DRAGON FROM
NEWSPAPER ADVERTISEMENTS
OR OVER THE INTERNET
NEVER, EVER BUY A DRAGON
FROM DOORSTEP SELLERS
ALWAYS CHECK PAPERWORK.
IF THERE ARE SUSPICIOUS BUMPS
OR TIPPEX MARKS ON THE
PAPER, REJECT THE DRAGON
ALWAYS
KEEP YOUR RECEIPT.

25

Chapter 5
Which Breed?

These are the four commonest breeds of dragon, but there are a multitude of mongrel variations (in addition to the Australian marsupial varieties). Bear in mind that, because of the secrecy of dragon-mating behaviour, most dragons are cross-breeds.

The Pit Blutgnasher

See illustration page 28

A huge, fearless bully boy of a dragon. Muscular neck and powerfully built limbs. Venomous saliva. Large, pointed fangs. Razor-sharp spines extending to the very tip of the tail. Cold, determined expression. Lightening reactions. Extraordinarily powerful flame-thrower. Inherently aggressive. A real dragon's dragon!

Diet must be carefully watched when young – some strains of blutgnashers can grow to 10 metres in length.

Eggs: large, pale and evenly shaped. Often faintly pulsating.

Flame range: 3 to 4 metres.

Medical Problems: None. Blutgnashers are super fit as well as super strong. They live a terribly long time and are virtually indestructible. This is not always an advantage.

Pros: Excellent guard dragons and a favourite with gangsters and criminals.

Cons: Blutgnashers require firm handling at all times. Also there is the size issue...

The Stumptailed Bolonka

See illustration page 31

A hardy, medium-sized, no nonsense dragon. Short yellow scales with brown freckles or blotches. Lazy, homeloving, very fond of drains. A nice serpent, if you don't mind smells.

Bolonkas are originally sewer dragons from Transylvania. They have spade shaped forepaws and extra strong claws for digging and tunnelling.

Because they have no tails, bolonkas won't knock down ornaments or swipe the books off a

shelf. But this is not a good dragon for the houseproud. No bolonka ever has clean talons. They are very messy eaters and hate soap.

Flame range: One metre

Eggs: Thick, misshapen shells often speckled or blotched.

Medical Problems: lice, warts, dandruff, haemorrhoids, lip rot, gum disease, intestinal worms, diarrhoea, crusty eyes, mouth ulcers, nasal polyps, bad breath, wind, peeling scales. Most bolonkas will harbour several minor infections at any one time.

Pros: A very economical dragon, there are always plenty of bolonka eggs on the market

Cons: Nasty personal habits. Bolonka boars have exceptionally pungent grease glands.

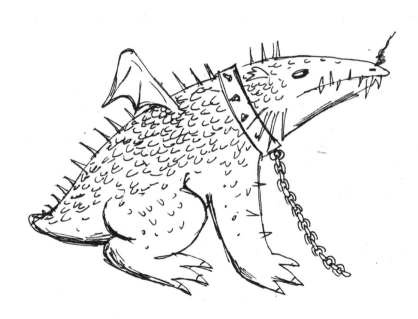

The Carpathian Schlange

See illustration page 33

A sturdy and sociable medium-sized dragon, ideal for family life. Thickset limbs, short stubby legs, large paws. Spade shaped face, bristly spines, needy expression.

Unlike most dragons, schlanges have feelings. They enjoy human contact and are the only breed known to weep while watching sad films on television. Very few schlanges end up as rescue dragons.

Schlanges love their food and will eat you out of house and home. Padlock the fridge and freezer. Do away with fruit bowls, do not

attempt to keep any food on open shelves. They love to go night foraging and must be locked up after sunset.

Eggs: very round shape, thick shell.

Flame Range: 1 to 1.5 metres

Medical Problems: indigestion, obesity.

Pros: a good beginner's dragon; schlanges will do anything for a morsel of food.

Cons: not a particularly clever dragon. Some dragon professionals complain that schlanges are soppy-they prefer a dragon with more grit to its character.

The Imperial Blue-Banded Squirrel-Dragon

See illustration page 35

A very small, very beautiful, premium dragon with refined tastes. Almond-shaped violet

eyes, and long shimmering scales, with characteristic bands of blue marking on the underbelly. The spines are long and frondlike and require daily brushing.

Squirrel-dragons are opinionated and demanding. They are prone to tantrums and sulks. They also are picky eater, and fussy about their jewellery/bedding. They hate draughts and demand continual pampering.

This is a high maintenance dragon. You will never be able to forget that you have a squirrel-dragon. You will marvel that a creature

so small can take up quite so much of your time.

Eggs: small and exquisite, slight blue tinge

Flame Range: 50 centimetres

Medical Problems: poor teeth, prone to fevers and fatigue, fainting fits, seizures, high blood pressure, very delicate.

Pros: a very decorative dragon that can fit in your handbag

Cons: can be spoilt and fretful. You will find the little scales get everywhere – on towels, under the doormat, in the butter dish.

Chapter 6
Your First Egg

Most people prefer to buy an egg. This is the most expensive option and there are risks: you can never be completely certain what will come out and, sadly, even dragons with great pedigrees can produce sparkless or deformed baby dragons. Also, you will have to be responsible for house-training your dragonlet.

On the other hand, if you buy an egg, you will be able to influence incubation and watch the shell develop and change colour. Nothing can match the excitement of a hatching!

Is it cruel to take an egg from its mother?

Dragons usually lay clusters of three or four eggs. Mother dragons get upset if all their eggs are removed, so the common practice is to leave one egg behind in the den for the mother to raise. Once this last egg has hatched and learnt to fly, it must be separated from its mother, who by then will be heartily sick of it. Breeders tend to do this very promptly – dragonlets that are left too long with their mothers normally get eaten.

How old should my egg be?

Dragon eggs take 6-12 months to hatch. For the first month, when the shell is still soft, they remain with their mother and the rest of the cluster. Any time after that is fine. As the egg matures it will gradually become hotter and change colour, turning from white to gold. For its

final week the egg turns red. We would not advise you to buy an egg immediately before hatching – in other words, a red egg or a gold egg significantly tinged with red. Any dragon egg needs time to settle down in its new environment.

Can I know the sex of my egg?

You can never be truly sure whether your egg will hatch into a dragon boar or a lady dragon. Some dragon dealers say they are able to tell the sex of an egg: they believe a long pointy egg is more likely to be male and a rounder egg will probably be female.

Others claim to be able to tell the sex by swinging a pendulum six inches above the egg. But this is all a very uncertain business.

What will my dragonlet look like?

Here too you are in the lap of the gods. Dragons mate in secret and hold the eggs in their bellies for years, so the father is nearly always a mystery. Your dragonlet may take after its mother, and a good dealer should be able to supply a photograph of mum. Egg size and markings should also give you some idea as to the breed or breeds involved. But every little dragonlet is different. Guessing is half the fun!

Is the shell shiny and smooth??

Is it a healthy egg?

Your egg should be shiny, evenly coloured and extremely hot to the touch.

Avoid cracked shells, flakey shells, eggs with uneven colouring.

How do I take my egg home?

Dragon eggs give off an extraordinary amount of heat and must be kept insulated at all times. Bring your den to the dragon breeder's shop. Encase the egg and surrounding treasure and jewellery in aluminium foil and then, very carefully, place the entire bundle directly into your dragon's new home.

Does it have a pearly translucency?

If possible check your egg's treasure for rubies or blood opals. These should be discreetly removed from the bedding. Red stones have been linked to temper tantrums in very young dragonlets.

You will be expected to return all jewellery after hatching.

How do I care for my egg?

Speak to your egg every day and keep it warm as toast. Reassure it. Put on your oven gloves and stroke it. Remember, you are now its mother.

If you want to have a gentle dragonlet, then play it classical music, folk songs, blues, jazz, recordings of whale songs.

If you spit on it, does it sizzle?

For a more spirited, lively dragonlet, try disco music, acid house, garage and hip-hop.

On *no account* play heavy metal – it may affect your dragon's mental health.

DRAGON DON'TS

- *Never* change your egg's treasure and jewellery.

You do not want your little dragonlet to become anxious.

- *Never* warm your egg up in the microwave.

- *Never* play football with your egg.

- *Never* put your egg in cold water.

Chapter 7

Your First Dragonlet

Buying a dragonlet is perhaps the safest and easiest option for first time dragon owners. You will not need to carry out basic training – your dragonlet should already able to fly, groom itself and use its dragon litter.

With a ready hatched dragonlet, there is also less risk of ending up with a sickly or sparkless dragon (mums tend to kill off weaklings shortly after hatching). But it is still important

to be vigilant. Always use a reputable dealer and choose your dragonlet very, very carefully.

PROFESSOR BLINK SAYS:
A DRAGONLET IS NEVER
LEFT ON THE SHELF WITHOUT
A VERY GOOD REASON.

When should I buy my dragonlet?

Dragon eggs tend to hatch during spring and are normally removed from the den at about ten weeks old, when they have learnt to fly and have received their first bites from mum. Dragonlets start to appear at dragon dealers in early June, with numbers peaking in September. Bargain hunters may want to wait for the end of season sales in November, but by then most quality stock has gone. Do not buy out of season, or overgrown dragonlets.

The show den

During peak season, dealers normally keep all their dragonlets together in one large show den. This allows you to get a proper sense of your dragonlet's personality and where they are on the pecking order.

TIP 1: dragonlets are not very kind to each other and these show dens can be gory places – bring some paper tissues to mop up any blood.

TIP 2: avoid the head of the pack – a very dominant dragon won't take orders from humans. And don't take pity on the smaller singed and wounded dragonlets quivering at the back of the den. Bullied dragons make terrible pets – later they will take revenge on you for their ill treatment. So, instead, harden your heart and choose a nice middle-of-the-road dragonlet – not too bossy, and not too self -pitying.

Picking the perfect dragonlet

Your dragonlet should have firm limbs, a good

snarl and a nice reddish-blue flame, like a medium-sized welding torch. But a dragonlet's temperament and responsiveness to humans is far more important than its looks.

Don't be in a hurry to choose your dragonlet. Stand at the front of the show den and wait and see. Sooner or later a little dragonlet should come forward, look you in the eye and then bite your fingers. Remember, biting is just a sign of interest. This may be the dragonlet for you!

Dragon boar or lady dragon?

Maybe you have set your heart on a lady dragon? Or (*this is less common*) on a dragon boar? Both sexes have their drawbacks.

Dragon boars are more boisterous and aggressive. They also tend to roam, and you will have to clean out their grease gland regularly (*see Good Grooming*).

Female dragons can be moody at times, and you must be prepared for the possibility that they will lay eggs. Female dragons are more likely to be whiney.

CHECK LIST

Is it a healthy dragon?

Do its eyes shine?

Is its snout burning hot?

Does it breath fire?
Do its limbs feel sturdy?

PROFESSOR BLINK SAYS:
NO TWO DRAGONLETS ARE ALIKE!
DRAGONLET BOARS CAN TURN OUT
TO BE VERY LADYLIKE, AND SOME
LADY DRAGONLETS ARE QUITE BOARISH.

Avoid dragonlets with moulting scales, dragonlets who sleep all the time, limp dragonlets. Your dragonlet should not be too large. See chapter 5 for information on breeds.

How do I take my dragonlet home?

Line your travelling cage with silk and velvet and scatter a few jewels on top. If you go by car or train rest the travelling cage on the seat beside you and talk quietly to your dragonlet. Explain where you live, who is in your family, and what other pets live in the house. You *must* stress that these pets are not food.

Tell your dragonlet that if he or she is very good, he or she will win rewards.

PROFESSOR BLINK SAYS: NEVER UNDERESTIMATE YOUR DRAGON!

What food should they be given?

Dragonlets tend to have delicate digestions, so don't change their diet overnight. Find out what your dragonlet has been eating up until now – most dealers will give you a few days supply of whatever biscuits the dragonlet has as a staple.

Will my dragonlet be homesick?

The sad truth is your dragonlet will be relieved to be away from the other dragonlets. It will be even more relieved to be away from Mum.

DRAGON DON'TS

■ *Never* pick a dragonlet up by
the tail.

■ *Never* taunt a dragonlet.

■ *Never* touch a dragonlet's wings-
though you can fondle their ears.

■ *Never* be tempted to buy two dragonlets
instead of one. If you do so you, you will end up
with just one dragonlet with a large stomach.

This family didn't follow my advice:

> Lark Rise Bunglaow,
> New Valley Estate,
> Chingbury

Hi Professor Blink,

I am one of triplets but we are all really, really, REALLY different. My name is Trinnie and I'm the tomboy. Little Tiffany is the girlie girl and wears pink. Theresa (we all call her Tubs) is pony mad.

When Mum and Dad said they would buy us a dragon for our birthday we said we just HAD to have one each. We hate joint presents. We each have our own clothes, our own toys, and our own toothbrushes. So why couldn't we have our own dragons?

Mum and Dad looked doubtful at first but we had a few tizzie fits and Tiff blubbed and in end they agreed-just like we knew they would.

So off we went shopping. The first two dragon dealers we visited were dead fussy and turned us away saying that they would never sell a family more than one dragon.

But then we visited this new dealer who was just, like, setting up shop and hadn`t been registered or anything. He wasn`t bothered. He said we could have as many dragonlets as we liked.

Tubs chose a nice sturdy Schlangelet and Tiff (predictable or wot!) went for a tiny Imperial Blue Whatever-you-call-it that was going to need TONS of grooming. I picked the biggest dragonlet -a really cool glossy Blutgnasher. He was a really fit dragonlet with slow, lazy sort of smirk.

That night we put all the dragonlets in their den. They took a while to settle down. There were a few shrieks and mewling sounds during the night, but by morning it was, like, DEAD quiet. When I went down to breakfast Tiff and Tub's dragonlets were lying in a little bundle at the back of the den. But my dragonlet was more perky. He sat at the front of the den, cleaning out his talons and burping.

We went off to school and when we came back... HEY! GUESS WOT? My dragonlet was moving around but Tiff's and Tubs' little serpies were STILL LYING IN A BUNDLE AT THE BACK. We looked a bit closer. It was SO dark at the back of the den and you couldn't make much out. But the Schlange and the tiny Whatever-you-call-it did seem a bit grey round the gills.

So we opened up the den and OH NO! You'll never believe It! They were BOTH dead, Dead, DEAD!

Tubs took it pretty well-she picked up her schlanglet, popped its entrails back in and got the spade out to bury it in the garden.

But Tiff really howled and snivelled and made her mascara run! I suppose you can't blame her—her Imperial Blue Thingummiebobbery had been a bit chewed. My blutgnasher must have found it quite tasty.

Now we only have one dragon. Tubs and Tiff don't want to touch him and I think I've gone off him a bit too.

Anyway, please tell everyone to stick to one dragonlet per family.

Yours and all that,
 Trinnie Jones

I have written to Trinnie asking for the name of her dealer. He will be reported to the Dragon Club!

Chapter 8

Rescue Dragons

Rescue dragons are dragons that have been returned to dealers by their owners. At first glance acquiring a rescue dragon may seem like the easiest option. There are always plenty of rescue dragons available and they are always cheap. In some cases dealers will pay you substantial sums to take a dragon off their hands!

But don't be fooled. A rescue dragon has usually been sent back to its dealer for a very good reason. And, unless you have a very experienced dragon handler in the house, you should not contemplate getting a rescue dragon. If you are under 12, you should **Definitely** not be anywhere near a rescue dragon. Leave this to the professionals.

Personally, I believe there should be a law against households with children owning rescue dragons. It is simply too dangerous. I admit that my own dragon, Picton, is a rescue dragon and that I have two children. But I have owned dragons since childhood (my mother was a dragon dealer) and I do enjoy a challenge. Also, I waited until my younger son was a stringy eight year old and no longer at all plump or juicy looking.

REMEMBER:

- Old dragons do not like to learn new tricks.
- Old dragons are faddy about food.
- Old dragons have expensive habits and tastes.
- Old dragons tend to be vicious.

Do you mind losing an eye/foot/hand/brother/sister?

If you still want a rescue dragon, always ask yourself:

1. Why is this dragon a rescue dragon?
2. Would you be very bothered if your house burnt down?
3. Do you want your neighbours to hate you?
4. Do you want to spend the rest of your life in prison?

Exceptions

Very occasionally dragons become rescue dragons through no fault of their own: their owners drop down dead, or suddenly they have to emigrate. **But these cases are very, very rare.** Decent, respectable dragons rarely end up as rescue dragons.

The Rescue Dragon

House of Horrors

The dragons described in this chapter have been making the rounds for some years.

If you do decide on a rescue dragon, please make sure that you avoid these particular dragons.

Grudgerella, 75 years old

A pit blutgnasher with grey underbelly, and characteristic blood red stripe down her back. Left wing missing (ripped off in the litter, a trauma from which she never recovered).

Grudgerella is a real killer – she once destroyed an entire herd of Friesian cows and has eaten small boats whole (crew included). She will attack when quite unprovoked and particularly loathes children. Many schools near her last den put up protective netting over their playgrounds.

Risk Rating: ***

Jojo *(aka Bloodfang, Arson Bill)* 82 years old

A pit blutgnasher easily recognisable by his double row of teeth. Jojo has extraordinary abilities as a flame thrower, but has never managed to control his temper.

Jojo has burnt down: two cinemas, three shopping malls, a circus, a whisky distillery, and countless shops selling fireworks. Jojo has a real weakness for explosions – the last match factory that he torched needed 12 fire-engines to put out the flames.

Risk Rating: ****

GR 636   7 years old

A plump, stumptailed bolonka, with very short talons. He should still have his police tag around his left forepaw.

Although still very young, GR 636 is the world's most destructive dragon. He would never harm a fly, but he can hack into any computer system and send it haywire. He has emptied bank accounts, derailed trains, crashed aeroplanes. His viruses have cost the government millions and millions of pounds.

GR 636 is very genial dragon, with a lovely smile. But he just can't help himself when it comes to computers.

Risk Rating: *****

Chardonnay 25 years old

A sparkless but otherwise fit Imperial blue-banded squirrel-dragon. Auburn hue, medium height, no distinguishing features.

Chardonnay is a born manipulator and an accomplished thief. She has weird psychic/mind reading powers. Even hardened dragon dealers are turned into quivering wrecks by Chardonnay and they never know quite how. Twelve children have run away from home after Chardonnay joined their families. She is also responsible for several mothers trying to jump under trains or drive their cars into walls.

Risk Rating: immeasurable

As this letter proves, you have to be a very special sort of person to run a home for rescue dragons. And the problems that arise can be quite surprising.

> North turret, Maclune Castle,
> Isle of Maclune,
> Very Outer Hebrides,
> Scotland

Hello Professor Blink!
My name is Ishbelle Macune of Maclune, and I live on the island of Maclune with my Dad, the Great One Handed Maclune of Maclune of Maclune. I am 14 and

I have never watched television or used a flushing toilet, but I am absolutely brilliant with difficult dragons. And I haven't lost a limb yet!

Castle Maclune, which is too damp ever to burn down, is the perfect place for dragons.
The boulders on the beach are covered in nutritious barnacles. And there is absolutely nothing else on the island – no houses, no trees, no jewellery shops. The ground is all blasted to a cinder. We are miles from anywhere. No one ever visits.

So dragons have been our life. We earn just enough from placement fees to keep us in tar and oatmeal. The dragons – at present there are 57 of them down in the dungeons – take the chill off the castle and we are quite used to the smell! Some of the younger dragons catch mice which I, ever since Dad carelessly lost his

right hand, skin and fillet. They make a nice change from porridge.

But a month ago everything changed with the arrival of Dougald. He was a truly rotten specimen - an undersized Pit Blutgnasher with a spiteful look in his eye. His Misdemeanours and Damages Report - mauling flocks of sheep, disemboweling owners and so on - was very bad.

He also had mange.

But, apart from a few fire blasts and lunges, Dougald went into his new dungeon quietly. I did notice that his owners had provided some quite unusual bedding treasure - a chess set, some packs of cards, a few rubic cubes - but I didn't think twice about it. Over the years I've seen some pretty surprising bedding treasure.

At first Dougald just snarled and farted in his

dungeon. Then, one lunchtime, I was throwing a few
boulders
into his dungeon when I noticed that he had carved
on the wall:
  What About A Game of Chess?
  I was a bit surprised he could write - and it was
in a very fancy copperplate paw. But dragons can be
very clever.
  Just by the entrance to the dungeon, he had set up
the chess board.
  I looked at Dougald. He winked.
  Then he checkmated me in four moves.
  The following day there was a new carving:
Poker (for mice)?
  Since then, we have played every game imaginable -
draughts,backgammon, poker, whist, rummy, bridge,
Black Maria, cribbage, Go...

Dougald has thrashed me at everything. He is, I soon realised, a two-brain dragon. He can do complex arithmetic in his head and has a photographic memory which allows him to remember every card that is played. He could win thousands in a casino.

I have quite enjoyed playing these games – it makes a nice change from counting seagulls. And now I understand the reason for Dougald's terrible behaviour in the past. He was just bored!

But Dougald is still discontented. He claims his talents are wasted here and he wants us to take him to Las Vegas, the gambling capital of the world...

Dad, who has never been off the island before, is very keen on the idea (he wants to buy a metal hook for his arm.) I feel more nervous. I do realise there could be more to life – the view from the fourth turret can get a bit boring. But I worry about our other 56 dragons. Also I suspect Dougald might get corrupted by the bright lights.

What do you think? Should we go?

From Ishbelle Maclune of Maclune,

(Dragon Trainer Par Excellence)

I wrote back to dear Ishbelle saying she should definitely take Dougald to Las Vegas.

Chapter 9

Hatching your Dragon

He needs stimulation.

Dragon eggs go through three distinct phases: the dormant period, transition, and hatching.

Phase One: the dormant egg

A freshly laid egg will have a white, closely grained shell. It will be hot to the touch, but not unbearably so. During this 'dormant'

period the little dragonlet inside will be deeply asleep and virtually dead to the world. The shell will also be nearly an inch thick which means you can do pretty much anything you like with the egg without it making much difference. But don't play football with it.

Phase Two: Transition

After 2 to 4 months your dormant egg will turn yellow. Your egg is now entering the second phase of its development, when the little dragonlet inside begins to wake up. The shell will now be beginning to thin out and the texture will become rougher. Your little

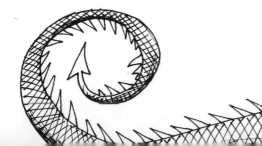

dragonlet will be particularly susceptible to sound and touch. (*The egg will be now be really heating up – you will need oven gloves from now on*).

During this developing phase, you should get working on your egg. Play music to your egg, stroke it, talk soothingly to it and turn it slightly every few hours. At this point all members of your household should talk regularly to the egg and take turns to gentle reposition it.

Family pets should also be encouraged to bark, miaow, chirrup or squeak regularly to the egg. This is very much in their interests. If the

dragonlet becomes familiar with them, it will learn that they are family members and not food.

Phase Three: The hatching.

First you will hear a drumming sound from inside the egg – that is the dragon trying to knock a hole in the shell with its beak. Suddenly there will be a loud crack, and a hiss of steam. When the steam clears you will see a small hole in the shell, and suddenly the tip of a little beak will stick out. There will be cracks down the side of the shell and the egg will now sway violently from side to side, as the dragonlet tries to break free. Eventually the egg will come crashing down on one side, smashing the shell to smithereens. And out of the wreckage will crawl your new dragonlet!

What do I do when the dragonlet comes out?

Your dragonlet will shiver and make pathetic mewling sounds. Wrap it in a towel and, using a warm damp cloth, gently unseal its eyes. Then use a hairdryer to fluff up its soggy scales. Your dragonlet will still be pretty groggy. Give it an egg-cup of brandy to cheer it up. But don't smile. You don't want to start out by giving your pet the upper hand.

Now stroke your dragonlet along its spines and tell it the rules of the household. You could say something like this, 'Hello little dragonlet. Welcome to our house. We are very pleased you survived incubation and I am sure we will have a lovely life together. This is your den, where you sleep and where you will go to the bathroom. You must not go to the bathroom anywhere else. You must not eat us or any part of us. You must only blow flames outside the house. Keep to these rules and we will all be friends.'

Then leave your dragonlet alone in its den to settle in. It will want privacy to eat its shell.

(All dragonlets do this – they need the calcium.)

Should my dragonlet really look like this?

Don't worry. All newly hatched dragonlets look terrible. It will perk up after you've dried its scales and given it a stiff drink. Then you must wait. In a couple of days your little creature will start to fill out and become recognisably dragonish. The scales will remain soft – a bit like the texture of astro turf – for at least a month.

DRAGON DON'TS

▪ *Never* use an egg piercer to encourage your dragonlet to hatch. *Nobody* likes to be rushed.

- **Never** take flash photographs during the hatching. It will enrage your dragonlet.

- **Never** pick up your egg or handle it during hatching. This will discombobulate your dragonlet. It has enough on its paws already.

Chapter 10
Feeding

Dragons are omnivores. That means they eat anything. They have extraordinarily strong, sharp teeth, and so can crunch their way through shell, bone, fruit stones, rubber tubing, etcetera. They also have a well developed sense of smell.

The mainstay of most dragon diet is dragon biscuits – a cup or one and a half cups (*depending on size*) three times a day. But what dragons really like is a varied and, above all, an **expensive** diet. They will eat almost anything if they think it will ruin you.

How do I give my dragon a healthy diet?

To keep its teeth sharp, a dragon must eat lots of crunchy food. So never cook its vegetables, or crack its nuts, or fillet its fish. If your dragon is to have tinned pilchards, just put the unopened can straight into its feeding bowl.

Feeding hatchlings

Day 1-3: Only bowls of warm milk

Day 4: Time for solids.

Start with white boiled rice.

Day 5-10: Introduce boiled buckwheat, mashed banana, lambs' liver.

Day10-21: You can now branch out: chicken, avocado, junior dragon biscuits.

Day 22. Feel free to try anything now. But there are some foods that even a fully grown dragon won't eat: broccoli, kale, gluten-free muesli.

What about dragon biscuits?

There are several varieties of dragon biscuits on the market and some more expensive brands – Supa Drago Crunch, Puff and Fang, Smaug's Original – advertise themselves as nutritionally complete. But dragons are not like dogs or cats or guinea pigs. They won't be happy if you feed them exactly the same food every day.

Always read the contents on the back of the bags. Avoid any bicuits containing sand and cement. Sand and cement may sharpen your dragon's teeth but they are building materials, not food. They will

make your dragon bloated and bad tempered and very blocked up.

Giant's Scalp

This pudding also doubles as an excellent hatching day cake. The brake fluid gives it a real kick and helps if your dragon suffers from bunged-up insides.

2 tins of fish paste (cheapest you can find)
2 dollops golden syrup
1lb oatmeal
3 tablespoonfuls of brake fluid
1-2 packet of liquorice shoestrings
I packet almond flakes

Mix together the fish paste, oatmeal, golden syrup, and brake fluid. Line a large, very round pudding bowl with clingfilm and place the mixture inside – it should be a disgusting pinky orange. Leave to set overnight.

The following day. Check the mixture has set and then upturn the bowl onto a plate. Remove the clingfilm. The mixture should be a horribly quivering dome.

Now place strands of liquorice shoestring (*the giant's hair*) across the mound. Finish off by sprinkling with almond flakes-that will be your giant's dandruff.

For a ginger giant scalp replace black liquorice with red.

Fake Caviar

Fake caviar is a staple for my Picton and it's cheap and easy to make for any occasion. The caviar forms a sweet, glistening, vinegary mass that he just adores.

The juice from one pickle jar
2 tablespoonfuls custard powder
Black food colouring
3 teaspoonfuls sugar

Heat up the pickle juice in a small pan. Add two tablespoonfuls of custard powder and a teaspoonful of black food colouring. Simmer

for five minutes then leave to cool. Sprinkle with sugar before serving.

Dragons love sweet and fishy combinations: liquorice allsorts mashed up with smoked mackerel, prawns in raspberry yoghurt, crème pilchard.

PROFESSOR BLINK SAYS:
NEVER GIVE YOUR DRAGON FOOD CONNECTED WITH FORESTS OR MOUNTAINS – IT REMINDS THEM OF THE HAPPY DAYS WHEN THEY LIVED IN THE WILD AND ATE US. SO NO BLACK FOREST GATEAU, NO MOUNTAIN SHAPED CHOCOLATE BARS.

DRAGON DON'TS

■ *Never* let your dragon over-indulge in: eggs, cabbage, goat's stew or prawn curry.

All these foods cause wind and can be **VERY DANGEROUS**. A build up in the system can cause blockage in the fire glands. If your dragon's pilot spark is extinguished, the fire glands will go into hyperdrive and start backfiring smoke into the body. This is called a smoke-out.

If untreated this condition can cause internal combustion. **Your dragon will explode!** That will be very upsetting and very messy. If your dragon starts to emit smoke from anywhere other than its nostrils, immediately dose it with an entire tin of bicarbonate of soda. Always keep some bicarbonate of soda in the kitchen and near the den.

■ **Never** dither. If you put food in the den, don't change our mind and try and take it out again. Your dragon will snap and you are guaranteed to lose a finger.

■ **Never** try to sneak medicines into their food.

■ **Never** ever forget to feed your dragon. They have long memories.

I always say that a dragon is an accident waiting to happen. This is particularly the case with dragons and cabbage. My dragon before Picton – a lovely little schlange, but a bit greedy – got loose on a cabbage patch and sadly exploded before we got to her.

But Helga's family were more fortunate:

Sunny Lea, Littlehampleton,

Dear Georgie Blink,

We have just made a COLOSSAL MISTAKE with our new dragon!
We let Maisie eat cabbage. She loved the stuff. She

IT WAS A SMOKE OUT!

ate it raw, fried, braised, boiled, and she didn't mind if it was green, white, red, yellow... She'd even have gobbled it down if it was tartan. She did seem a bit burpy, but, as she is our first dragon, we didn't think too much about it.

But then last week we had our German Evening. Mum cooked sauerkraut which is a German speciality, a sort of pickled cabbage that you eat with boiled meats.

Maisie ADORED it. Her eyes went all glazey. She had seconds, and thirds, and fourths and fifths. In the end, after the saucepan had been scraped completely clean, Maise curled up in the corner of her den, closed her eyes and started to fart.

Later we all went to bed as usual, and luckily mum had opened the window in the utility room.

The fire alarm woke me at midnight. I was the first out of bed. I went downstairs and this creepy curtain of thick black smoke was slowly coming up the stairs towards me. It felt like something out of Lord of the Rings, but I took a big breath and ran down into the hall and opened the kitchen door.

The air was absolutely black with smoke and Maisie was thrashing around on the floor, with her eyes rolled backwards. All that evil black smoke was pouring out of her nostrils and her armpits and, especially, her bottom.

Luckily I had read the What To Do In An Emergency section of your guide. I grabbed a tin of bicarbonate of soda and, while Mum forced Maisie's mouth open with a pair of tongs, I emptied the powder down her throat. The smoke stopped immediately. Maise's shoulders suddenly drooped, and her eyes swivelled back into place. Then, completely dazed and worn out, she fell fast asleep.

Maisie's teeth are now black, and so are her nostrils and ear cavities. But-here is the good news – her droppings are also pitch black and give off smoke. Our dealer says that smoked out dragon droppings are worth their weight in weapons-grade uranium! He has paid us so much money that we can pay the dental hygienist and redecorate the entire house and still have enough left over for a holiday abroad.

So it's not all bad. My money grabbing little brother, now he has realised we can make a profit with the droppings, wants us to stage another German night.

And Maisie's very keen. She would kill for pickled cabbage. If you even mention the word 'sauerkraut' she starts to leak smoke.

But hey! We have all survived!

Helga

Maisie's little brother had better watch out! I have my eye on him!

Chapter 11

Understanding your Dragon

Dragons are not like dogs – you can't tell their mood by just watching to see if they wag their tails. With dragons, you must examine their faces, their tails, their scales, the lie of their ears and spines, the colour of their smoke. Dragons also show their mood in a thousand other subtler ways – from how they puff, to how they flick their tail. But that varies with the individual.

New dragon owners may find the idea of decoding their dragon a bit daunting. It seems like a lot to take in. But everything will soon become second nature. With time you will know your dragon so well that you'll register its mood without even having to think about it.

In the meantime here is a rough guide:

The Happy Dragon

Half closed shining eyes, glossy scales, relaxed spines, wagging tail, ears flat, steady gentle puffs of smoke

The Angry Dragon

Thickened, retracted neck, raised
scales, ears pricked up, rigid,
glaring eyes, fangs bared, wing
bridges extended.
Thick black smoke. Sparks.
Unretracted claws drumming
repeatedly on the ground.
Tail rigid and upright.

The Frightened Dragon

Back arched,
spines pricked up,
ears pricked up,
scales ruffled.
Head twists away in fear,
weight on back paws.
Faint mewling sound.

The Dragon that Wants Something

Lowered head, lowered spines, ears flat, flushed
underbelly, wheedling expression, gentle
puffs of white smoke, curled tail.

The Guilty Dragon

Ears flat,
bloody claws,
food deposits around mouth,
full belly, thick black smoke,
eyes downcast and probably
busy examining talons.
Tuneless whistle.

The Ill Dragon

Dull eyes, sad expression, lifeless posture, ears flat,
moulting scales, palid smoke. No sparks.

The Dead Dragon

Greyish complexion, open mouth,
ears flat, blank
expression.
No smoke.
No sparks.

100

Chapter 12

Dragon Training

There are three basic rules you want to instil in your dragon:

1) Don't eat any person or pet in the family.
2) Don't steal jewellery
3) Don't set fire to the home.

Remember that dragons are very clever. They never have problems understanding. They are far more intelligent than other animals (including humans). They also understand all languages – even dead ones like Latin, or obscure ones like Manx. (Try this out – find, say, a Tibetan phrase book and murmur something very rude to your dragon in Tibetan. Watch its spines rise.)

So you'll never have trouble getting your dragon to understand. With a dragon, the problem is always one of making it **WANT** to obey. If, for example, you throw the ball into the air and shout 'fetch,' your dragon will probably just roll its eyes and slump its wing bridges and blank you. But if you say 'fetch the ball and it'll be champagne and oysters for supper **AND** I'll lend you Dad's iPod,' your dragon will fetch that ball faster than greased lightning.

How do I make my dragon want to obey me?

Fear can be useful, though your approach has to be subtle (see Paul the Bad Dragon p107). And by all means use bribery. Dragons are greedy; lady dragons will do anything for small items of jewellery and dragon boars adore trombone music. Always be generous with your bribes. Don't try and fob your dragon off with a slither of ripe French cheese. Give it a huge chunk.

But, on their own, fear and bribery are not enough. You must earn your dragon's respect. Your dragon must believe that you are

cleverer and more ruthless than it. You will need to be quick witted. You will need to be devious. Above all, you will need to be strong.

The Upper Hand — You Are Top Dragon!

Your dragon must realise that he is at the bottom of the pecking order. So always feed your dragon after yourself, never let him or her go through a door before you, never let him sit on the chair nearest to the fire.

At all times you must appear in control. If you are feeling weepy or fragile, stay away from your dragon. Or, if you absolutely have to go near the den, at least wear dark glasses.

If your dragon blasts smoke in your face, never pretend it didn't happen.

If your dragon jostles past you, be quick to punish. Don't let yourself be snubbed.

Never ignore an insolent look. Rudeness is not acceptable. Ever.

PROFESSOR BLINK SAYS:
IF YOU GIVE YOUR DRAGON AN INCH IT WILL TAKE A MILE.

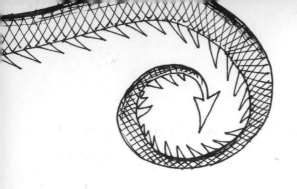

Punishments

At all times remember that you are the boss. If your dragon misbehaves withdraw food, withdraw treats, withdraw stimulae. Some dragon owners punish their dragons by making them swallow ice cubes, but this is cruel and can lower their combustibility.

Don't threaten your dragon and on no account hit it. Dragons harbour grudges for a very long time.

If everything goes completely pear-shaped

you may have to resort to returning your dragon to your dealer. Then it will be time to recoup, debrief, think hard and – hopefully – start again.

Mind Game 1: Paul the Bad Dragon

Always pretend that your first dragon is really your second dragon. Invent a pet dragon that behaved really badly and was sent away. Give him a name (let's call him 'Paul') and invent some awful things that he did. Every few days mention him and his dreadful deeds in your dragon's presence. Shake your head sadly and say 'Poor Paul. If only he hadn't eaten that cat...' Or 'I did warn Paul, but he just wouldn't listen...' If your dragon's ears always prick up at the mention of Paul, you will know that the trick is working.

Never say exactly what happened to Paul. You have to keep your dragon guessing.

Mind Game 2: Chess

Teach your dragon chess one evening when it is feeling slightly tired. Explain the rules very quickly and in as garbled a fashion as possible. Then set up the board. Don't be forgiving. Thrash your dragon, take every piece you can. Express surprise that he or she doesn't seem to have mastered the rules.

Pick up a book or a magazine and pretend to read it while you are playing – as if you had lots of spare brain unoccupied by the process of playing chess. Then you can save face if the dragon does begin to beat you.

The important point is that you must win – for your dragon has to believe you are a genius. If it looks as if your dragon will beat you then you have to bluff your way out. The best method is to resign quickly. Your dragon will then look at you questioningly. You reply 'Well it's obvious isn't? You will beat me twelve moves from now.'

The same techniques can be used with other board games.

Dragons are Devious!

Never give your dragon room to manoeuvre. If you say, 'You mustn't steal Mum's jewellery,' then your dragon will nod solemnly and, in a flash, it will be ripping the pearl necklace off your elderly aunt. Instead you have to say 'You mustn't steal Mum's jewellery or jewellery belonging to anybody else.'

Similarly it is not enough to tell your dragon, 'Don't eat the pet guinea pigs.' You also have to add 'or the neighbour's guinea pigs or the neighbours pet rats, or – for that matter – the neighbour.' Inevitably you won't always get this right. We made a terrible mistake with Picton. We drew up an incredibly long list of all the local pets that he must not eat. We even remembered to add hedgehogs and obscure breeds of lizard. But we forgot about the exquisite little chinchilla at number 12. The neighbours have still not forgiven us.

Don't let your Dragon:

Hang around the bathroom.
Play with the toilet brush.
Scorch the walls.
Melt your toys.
Raid the fridge.
Frighten the neighbours.
Fart into the fire.
Monopolise the most
comfortable chair in the house.
Go on the internet.
Get access to credit cards.
Bully or eat the cat/dog/
rabbit/guinea pig.
Interfere with low
flying aircraft.

Toilet Training Newly Hatched Dragonlets

Scatter a few dung pellets (your dealer should provide training pellets free of charge) in your droppings tray. Your dragonlet will understand immediately. Congratulate and stroke your dragon the first time it uses its tray. (*Don't overdo this – your dragon is no fool.*)

If your dragon does his business anywhere else this should be treated as active disobedience and punished.

DRAGON DON'TS

- **Never** say 'Aren't you a clever little dragon?' Or 'Good Girl!'

Dragons have dignity. They want to be addressed on an equal footing. Never make your dragon sit up and beg for treats.

- **Never** try to appeal to their sense of fairness.

- **Never** accept excuses.

Even if a dragon is tired, it can still retrieve a ball from a tree.

- **Never** , ever let your dragon watch the television shopping channels.

This couple want to break every rule of dragon husbandry. Where do you start when you get a letter like this?

Sunshine Treehouse,
The Peace and Love Commune,
Loveshire

Dear G. Blink,
Fern and I have decided to buy a dragonlet and call her Petal.
We believe that rules restrict inner growth.

So instead we want to nurture her with love and kindness. There will be no padlock for our Petal, and no den. At night she will share our bed and in the morning she will wake to the sound of our wind chimes and spend her day relaxing on her embroidered cushion. Instead of treasure she will have crystals and scented candles to help her find her inner calm. For amusement she can frolick in the green meadow beneath our treehouse.

We believe that dragons have been misunderstood. Like every creature on this universe, they are free spirits. Are we not all children of the rainbow?

I know this will seem a little different from your approach, but we would appreciate your advice.

What breed of dragon would you recommend us to start out with? (In the future we hope to branch out and have several little dragonlets frolicking in our meadow).

Peace, love and blue skies.

River Openheart

I advised Fern and River to buy a very large Pit Blutgnasher! I have not heard from them again.

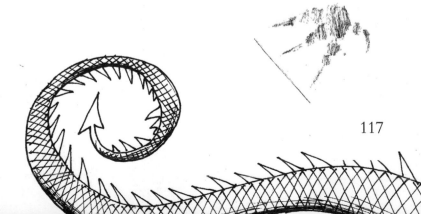

Chapter 13

Good Grooming

Some dragons are naturally clean. But most are, well, not so clean. Your dragon may groom itself, trim its own talons, and descuff, buff and polish of its accord. But self-grooming dragons are rare.

Do I have a self-grooming dragon?

You probably don't. But it's easy to check.

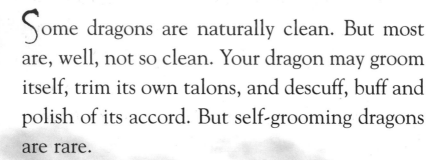

First, having put on your gloves and mask, gently sniff your dragon. Don't worry - you only have to press your nose against the dragon for a millesecond. But this should be long enough for you to decide. A nice clean dragon smells of burnt matches and old haddock pie. The smell of a dirty dragon is almost indescribable and certainly unprintable.

If you are still not sure, examine your dragon's grease gland. *(This only applies to dragon boars)*. The grease gland is a small oval shaped bump on the underside of the dragon's tail, near the tip. If the gland is black and emits a pungent odour then it will require cleaning. Some older dragons were docked as dragonlets and therefore have no tip to their tail and no grease gland. But nowadays docking is considered to be cruel. Few vets carry out this operation.

Grooming Your Dragon

Step 1. Prepare your grooming station.

On a flat surface lay down plenty of newspaper and aluminium foil. Put out your grooming aids — grooming brush, tweezers, cotton buds, scale polisher, buffing cloth, several disposable dishcloths, clippers. You will also need a small basin of hot soapy water. Have the fire-extinguisher and fire blanket nearby.

Step 2. Pick up your dragon. In a cheerful but firm voice tell your dragon it is about to be groomed. Ignore all snarls and put on your mask and oven gloves. Then, holding your dragon by the back of the neck with one hand, place your other hand under its bottom. Pick your pet up and settle it on the grooming station. Don't loose your nerve. Even if your dragon fights back you must not give up at this point!

PROFESSOR BLINK SAYS:
HANDLE YOUR DRAGONLET
EVERY DAY, EVEN IF YOU
GET BURNT OR BITTEN.

Step 3. The grease gland. This is the messiest job. Gently lift your dragon's tail, wipe the paper towel carefully over and around the grease gland. On contact with the paper towel the gland will spurt out a black noxious grease. Discard the paper towel. Start again. You may have to use several towels before the gland and surrounding area is clean.

Step 4. Brushing and descuffing. Using one hand to keep your dragon still, start brushing your dragon's back, working down the body using long, swift brush strokes. Then brush under the chin and round the belly. Hold the dragon's forepaws to complete the underside.

Finish off with a quick brush all round to get rid of any loose scales. If there are still scuff marks left on the scales, take a damp cloth and wipe them off.

Step 5. Polishing. Put a small amount of polish on a paper towel and, again working down the body of your dragon, gently smooth the scales. Pay particular attention to the softer underbelly area.

Step 6. Talons, ears and nostrils. You should now wait ten minutes for the polish to soak in. (Try your best to stop the dragon licking all the polish off.) You can use this time to clip back any overgrown talons and clean the nostrils and ears with cotton buds. Normally the nostrils will be very sooty.

Step 7. Buffing. Working from the nose downwards, rub your dragon's scales with a soft, clean buffing cloth. You'll be amazed just how sleek and shiny your dragon now looks!

Skin shedding – why is my dragon being so difficult?

Your dragon will shed its skin about every six months. Dragonlets, because they are outgrowing their skins faster, will shed more frequently.

You will know when your dragon is about to shed its skin because it will rub its back against the walls of the den and become bloated and grumpy. Try to be understanding: the mood swings are caused partly by discomfort (imagine how you would feel if your skin was one size too small) and partly by hormonal changes.

But, however hard you try, there will still be rows, wounds, scorchings.... You will be wondering why you ever bothered to get a dragon, and for the first few sheddings you will probably be beginning to devise a plan to be free of your wretched pet. Then one morning you will come to breakfast and find the air has cleared. There, lying in a crumped heap in a corner of the den, will be the old skin. And resting by its side will be a fresh, happy dragon with gleamings scales. All will be forgiven. Then, after a few months, the cycle will begin again....

My dragon hates being groomed, what should I do?

Some owners find that their dragons can be kept calmer with soft music and low lighting. Personally I groom my Picton in the sitting room, so that he can watch television while I brush and buff.

Certainly you should always talk softly to a dragon while you groom it. Do not whistle or hum tunes – you are not washing a car.

If you are still having problems you might want to invest in a grooming clamp. (*See Dragon Products*)

How often should I groom my dragon?

This is entirely up to you. Try once a week, or as often as you can face.

How do I clean my Dragon's teeth?

It is simply not safe to try and brush your dragon's teeth. Mouthwash is also out of the question. Dragons love the stuff, but they just gulp it straight down.

So, sooner or later, you will probably have to visit a dragon dentist. Here your dragon will have to have a general anaesthetic before any work can begin.

Top dragon dentist
Heronimous Wermclean speaks:

Cleaning dragon's teeth is a skilled procedure. Firstly we fire an anaesthetic needle into the dragon's rear and wait ten minutes for the drug to take effect. Then, with a couple of small power drills we attack the yellow encrustation on the external side of the teeth. Using a hammer and chisel we remove any scaling on the back molars.

Then, dressed in protective suits, we spray the inside of the mouth with bleach. We close the dragon's mouth and, having placed the dragon on a small trampoline, bounce it up and down to ensure the liquid penetrates all the crevices.

Sometimes, if the scaling is very thick, we

use a low level explosive, though we leave this for last because you do then run the risk of waking up the dragon.

You must, I insist, MUST bring your dragon to us regularly.

Never forget: bright, shiny fangs are what every dragon deserves!

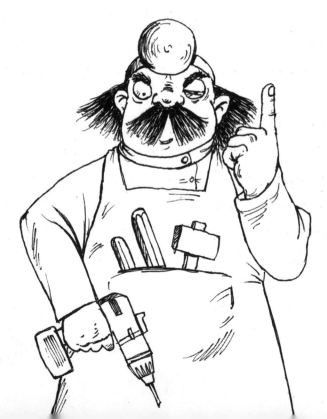

Scale Rot or Boggy Wing

Because of the warmth generated by dragons, they have a tendency to get fungal infections. If you notice a whitish deposit under the scales, visit the vet.

Dragon Don'ts

- *Never* attempt cleaning a dragon that will soon be shedding its skin. This is a waste of time.

- *Never* brush your dragon's scales in the wrong direction.

- *Never* bath your dragon.
Dragons hate water and it isn't good for them

- *Never*, EVER brush your dragon's teeth.

I was shocked to receive this letter!

Bullybeef Barracks,
Windybog Moor
Windybog

Dear Prof.

We used to have a terrible time trying to groom our Susie. We tried clamps, we tried tying her up, we tried filling her with whisky. But nothing worked. She would just go wild - even at the sight of the grooming brush.

We were getting desperate and the fug in the utility room was bad, **bad**, **BAD.**

So I thought I would try something different. I went to the armaments store and borrowed a nifty little triple action 80,000 volt stun-gun with energizer alkaline batteries. The gun sends a massive electric shock through the body and is a VERY POWERFUL WEAPON.

Well, one day when the missus was out (she doesn't love guns the way I do), I tried it out. It did the job! Susie was out cold in a flash. In fact it was BRILLIANT! Now, once a week, I just creep up behind Susie, aim the stun gun and WHAM!!! I have twenty minutes when she is out cold and I can polish her and spit n' buff till you can see your reflection in her scales. So everybody is now happy. I've resisted the temptation to use the stun gun on our terrible twins Sean and Ryan. But only just...

Yours, Sergeant-Major Bob Bullybeef

PS Susie isn't quite so friendly and trusting as she used to be. Any thoughts?

I have, of course, reported Sergeant-Major Bullybeef to the National Society for the Protection of Dragons.

Chapter 14

What to do in an Emergency!

Help! My dragon has black smoke pouring out of it in every direction.

This is a smoke-out. Your dragon is suffering from a build up of smoke in its combustion system. You must act quickly. Go to your kitchen cupboard and find a tin of bicarbonate of soda (it is used in baking cakes). Pour all the powder down your dragon's mouth. If there's no bicarbonate of soda, use sherbet. If there is no sherbet, use soap powder (but that can lead to more bubbles...)

The dragon has bitten off my hand. What should I do?

Pick up the bitten off limb (do not put the severed hand in ice), lock up the dragon and leave the room. Call the emergency services. **Do NOT** put your other hand into the den.

My dragon has started to bite its own tail. What is the problem?

There are occasional cases of mental illness among dragons, but it is much more likely that your pet is simply a bit bored.

Problem Case Study One.

My dragonlet, who is just learning to fly, is scared of heights.

This morning she flew up to the roof of the house but then promptly lost her nerve. She is still up there now clutching onto the television ariel and mewing pathetically. How do I get her down?

She should be getting hungry. Buy a chunk of Gorgonzola cheese or a small slice of beef fillet and try waving it in her direction. If that fails, call the fire - brigade.

Problem Case Study Two.

My mum's jewellery has disappeared .
The lock of the jewellery box has been broken and there are deep scratches down the side. Sigmund just shakes his head and bellows out smoke every time I ask him about it. He also won't come out of his den. What should I do?

Sigmund won't come out of the den because he is, of course, sitting on your mum's jewellery. Dragons are very clever about everything else in life, but they are never good at hiding their treasure. It is as if they can't help themselves - they just **HAVE** to sit on it.

You have two choices. You can stop feeding him until he owns up, but he may get very, very thin before that happens. Or you can try a different tack. Tell Sigmund it doesn't matter about the missing jewellery. Then say – in a resigned tone of voice – that you had thought he was a clever, discerning dragon. Add that you are most disappointed in him – for you thought that all dragons could tell the difference between fake gems and the real thing. Then reassure him. Say he mustn't worry – making new copies of the original jewels in your mother's bank vault should be easy and will only take a few weeks.

This should unnerve him.

Chapter 15

Dragon Products

The Kumfy Grooming Clamp

A sturdy, durable stand to help fix your dragon for easy grooming. Stable, fireproof stainless steel stand, easy-to-use head vice, two hinged body rings, four gently padded nylon cuffs, retractable tail stabiliser. Available in small (50cm x 23cm), medium (75cm x 40cm), large (120cm x 50cm). Self-assembly.

The Beelzebub Muzzle

An aid to calm and control boisterous and fiery dragons. This soft-but-strong muzzle has a custom-moulded asbestos mesh to prevent chaffing and suffocation. Fast and easy to fix, even with gloves on. Fitting service available. Otherwise snout length and nostril-to-nostril measurements required. For premier models please specify jewel encrustation. Next day delivery.

Camelot Snick-Snacks

Your dragon will love these crunchy novelty biscuits. Only 55 percent fat and coated in delicious maiden's blood, Camelot Snick-Snacks come in a classic collection of shapes including: castles, princesses, crowns, maces, knights in armour. Biscuit base contains mint, eucalyptus and drain cleaner for fresher breath.

Twenty Questions to Test Your Knowledge: Are you a dragon expert?

1) Before your dragon comes home you must buy
   a) a bag of white mice
   b) a sturdy padlock
   c) a one way ticket to New Zealand

2) What music should you NEVER play to your dragon egg?
   a) rock and roll
   b) heavy metal
   c) medieval chanting

3) What will your dragonlet feel
about being taken from its mother?
   a) anger
   b) sadness
   c) sheer relief

4) Before picking up a dragon you should:
   a) put on oven gloves
   b) have a cup of tea
   c) pray

5) If you use sequins in your
dragon's bedding your pet will begin to:
   a) twinkle
   b) get skin infections
   c) take up sewing

148

6) A dragon boar's grease gland is:
   a) on the tip of its nose
   b) under its chin
   c) on the underside of its tail

7) When cleaning a dragon's ears, what do you use?
   a) a long pointed stick
   b) a cotton bud
   c) a power hose

8) Which food should you NEVER give to your dragon in excess?
   a) cabbage
   b) ravioli
   c) lemon sherbet

9) Dragons usually lay clusters of:

a) three to four eggs

b) twelve to fifteen eggs

c) 99 eggs

10) The smelliest breed of dragon is a:

a) Pit Blutgnasher

b) Imperial Blue-Banded Squirrel-Dragon

c) Stumptailed Bolonka

11) The breed of dragon most likely to whine at mealtimes and leave its fish heads at the side of the plate is a:

a) Stumptailed Bolonka

b) Imperial Blue-Banded Squirrel - Dragon

c) Carpathian Schlange

12) The breed of dragon that will eat your uncle Lionel and not even bother to spit out his pipe and glasses is a:
 a) Carpathian Schlange
 b) Pit Blutghasher
 c) Stumptailed Bolonka

13) Before an egg hatches it turns:
 a) yellow
 b) purple
 c) red

14) Dragon boars are particularly fond of:
 a) cream buns.
 b) cardboard boxes.
 c) trombone music.

15) If your dragon bites off your hand you should:

a) place your other hand in the den.

b) give your dragon extra food – it must have been hungry.

c) call an ambulance.

16) A dragon's tail sticks straight up when it is:

a) angry

b) surprised

c) having trouble with its digestion

Answers: 1b, 2a, 3c, 4a, 5b, 6c, 7b, 8a, 9a, 10c, 11b, 12b, 13a, 14c, 15c, 16a

How Did You Score?

1-3 Pitiful! You shouldn't be allowed within 30 metres of a dragon egg!

4-6 Poor. You are still not well enough informed to keep your own dragon.

7-9 Okayish. You could still do better – please reread this book.

10-12 Good. But remember attention to detail is important if you are to do your best by your dragon

13-16 Well done! I could hire you tomorrow as my assistant dragon - carer.

Dragon Gallery,
Can you identify these breeds?

157

158

Go to www.professorblink.co.uk
and check your answers

Index